This notebook belo

MW00897759

Hello 你好 nǐ hǎo

Each page in **Chinese For Kids Practice Notebook 1 inch Grids Tian Zi Ge** Cat Edition has 100 pages of 35 blank grids with tian zi ge dashed lines to guide strokes. Whimsical cats and a school of fish are ready to join your child's writing journey.

Ask your child to grade their own writing by checking the stars in the top corner of each page.

Practice writing pages are best used with pencils, colored pencils, pens and crayons.

Use the grids below to test your writing tool.

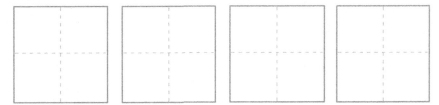

Thank you for choosing **Chinese For Kids Practice Notebook 1 inch Grids Tian Zi Ge** for your child's learning adventure!

Chinese For Kids Practice Notebook 1 inch Grids Tian Zi Ge
ISBN-13: 978-1722847555
ISBN-10: 1722847557

Let's Practice Writing

Name	Date

Name	Date

Name

Date

Let's Practice Writing

Let's Practice Writing

Name	Date

Let's Practice Writing

Name	Date

me				Date

Name	Date

Let's Practice Writing

Name	Date

Let's Practice Writing

Name	Date

t's Practice Writing ★★★

Name

Date

Let's Practice Writing

| Name | Date |

Let's Practice Writing

Name	Date

Let's Practice Writing

Name	Date

me	Date

Let's Practice Writing

Name	Date

Let's Practice Writing

Name	Date

Let's Practice Writing

Name	Date

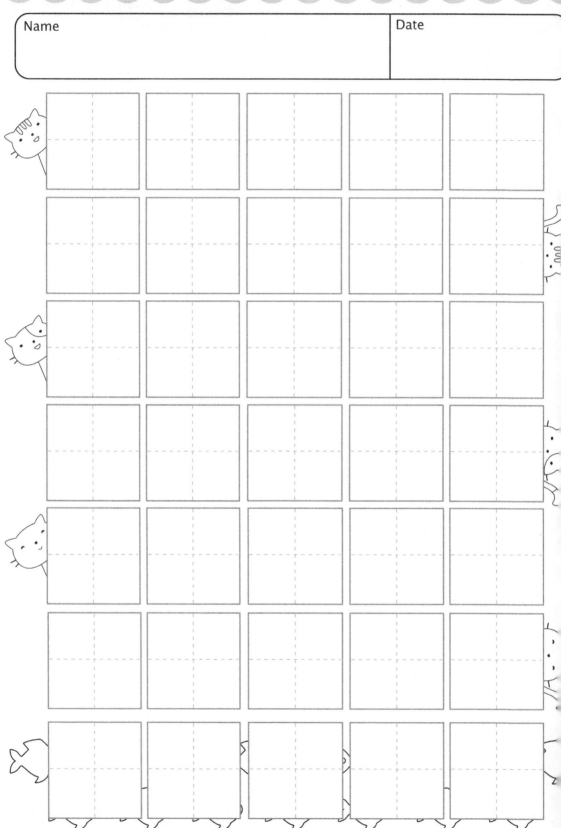

me		Date	

Let's Practice Writing

Name	Date

Name	Date

Name	Date

Name

Date

Let's Practice Writing

Let's Practice Writing

Name		Date

Let's Practice Writing

Name	Date

me

Date

Let's Practice Writing

Let's Practice Writing

Name	Date

Name

Date

Let's Practice Writing

| Name | | Date |

Name	Date

Let's Practice Writing

Name	Date

Name

Date

Let's Practice Writing

Name	Date

Let's Practice Writing

Name	Date

Let's Practice Writing

Name	Date

's Practice Writing

Name

Date

Let's Practice Writing

Name	Date

Name				Date

Let's Practice Writing

me

Date

Let's Practice Writing

Name	Date

Let's Practice Writing

Name

Date

Let's Practice Writing

Name	Date

Let's Practice Writing

Name	Date

Let's Practice Writing

Name	Date

Name

Date

Let's Practice Writing

Name	Date

Let's Practice Writing

Name	Date

Let's Practice Writing

Name	Date

's Practice Writing

Name

Date

Let's Practice Writing

Name	Date

Name

Date

Name	Date

Name

Date

Name				Date

Name	Date

Let's Practice Writing

Name	Date

:'s Practice Writing

Name

Date

Let's Practice Writing

Name	Date

Name				Date

Let's Practice Writing

Name		Date

Name

Date

Let's Practice Writing

Name	Date

Name	Date

Let's Practice Writing

Name

Date

me

Date

Let's Practice Writing

| Name | Date |

| Name | Date |

Let's Practice Writing

| me | | | | Date |

Let's Practice Writing

Name	Date

Name	Date

Name	Date

Name

Date

Let's Practice Writing

Name	Date

Name

Date

Let's Practice Writing

Name		Date	

Name

Date

Let's Practice Writing

Name	Date

Name

Date

Let's Practice Writing

Name	Date

Name

Date

Let's Practice Writing

Name	Date

Name	Date

Let's Practice Writing

| Name | Date |

Name

Date

Name	Date

Name

Date

Let's Practice Writing

Name	Date

Name

Date

Name	Date

Name	Date

Name	Date

Name

Date

Check Out Our Workbooks

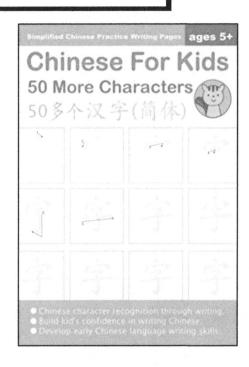

Free Worksheets

Free worksheets and book reviews are available on our official website:

www.adoreneko.com

Made in the USA
Las Vegas, NV
08 October 2023